Suzuki®

BASS SCHOOL

Volume 4
Piano Accompaniment

AMPV: 1.00

© 2015, 2008 Dr. Shinichi Suzuki
Sole publisher for the entire world except Japan:
Summy-Birchard, Inc.
Exclusive print rights administered by Alfred Publishing Co., Inc.
All rights reserved Printed in USA

ISBN-10: 0-7390-4879-1
ISBN-13: 978-0-7390-4879-5

INTRODUCTION

FOR THE STUDENT: This material is part of the worldwide Suzuki Method® of teaching. The companion recording should be used with this publication. In addition, there are bass part books that go along with this material.

FOR THE TEACHER: In order to be an effective Suzuki teacher, ongoing education is encouraged. Each regional Suzuki association provides teacher development for its membership via conferences, institutes, short-term and long-term programs. In order to remain current, you are encouraged to become a member of your regional Suzuki association, and if not already included, the International Suzuki Association.

FOR THE PARENT: Credentials are essential for any teacher you choose. We recommend you ask your teacher for his or her credentials, especially those relating to training in the Suzuki Method®. The Suzuki Method® experience should foster a positive relationship among the teacher, parent and child. Choosing the right teacher is of the utmost importance.

To obtain more information about the Suzuki Association in your region, please contact:

International Suzuki Association
www.internationalsuzuki.org

CONTENTS

1
Theme from the Mahler Symphony No. 1

G. Mahler
Piano accompaniment arranged by
Domenick Fiore

2

Chorus from "Judas Maccabaeus"

G. F. Handel

3
Die Meistersinger

Richard Wagner
Piano arranged by
Virginia Dixon

8

4

Tempo di Polacca

(Etude # 17)

Franz Simandl
Piano acc. Charlotte Durkee

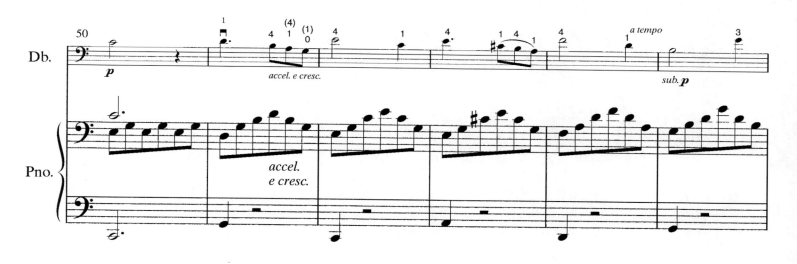

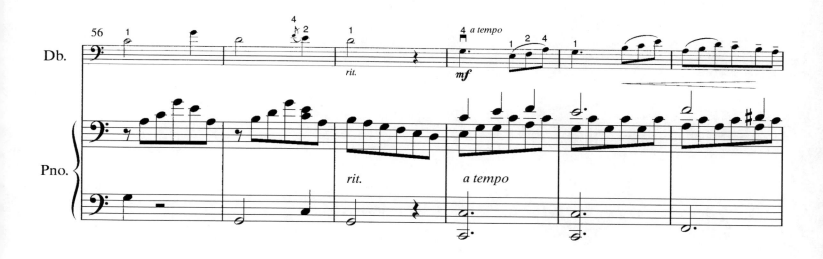

5
Gavotte in G minor

J. S. Bach

6
La Cinquantaine

Gabriel-Marie

7
Humoresque

A. Dvořák

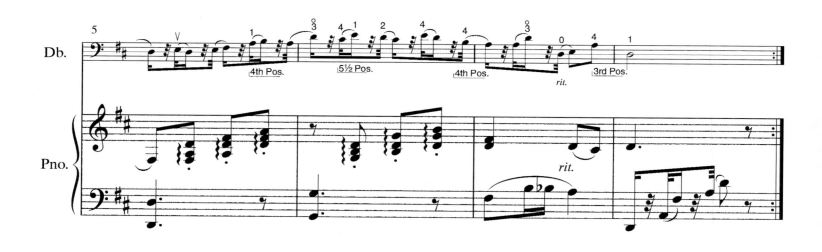

This page has been left blank intentionally to facilitate page turns.

8

Sonata in E minor,

Op. 1, No. 2

Benedetto Marcello

26